Antonio López de Santa Anna

Consulting Editors

Hispanics of Achievement

Antonio López de Santa Anna

Steven O'Brien

Chelsea House Publishers
Philadelphia

CHELSEA HOUSE PUBLISHERS

Editor-in-Chief: Remmel Nunn
Managing Editor: Karyn Gullen Browne
Copy Chief: Mark Rifkin
Picture Editor: Adrian G. Allen
Art Director: Maria Epes
Assistant Art Director: Howard Brotman
Manufacturing Director: Gerald Levine
Systems Manager: Lindsey Ottman
Production Coordinator: Marie Claire Cebrián

Hispanics of Achievement
Senior Editor: John W. Selfridge

Staff for ANTONIO LÓPEZ DE SANTA ANNA
Copy Editor: Christopher Duffy
Designer: Robert Yaffe
Picture Researcher: Diana Gongora
Cover Illustration: Danny O'Leary

5   7   9   8   6

Library of Congress Cataloging-in-Publication Data
O'Brien, Steven.
    Antonio López de Santa Anna/Steven O'Brien.
        p. cm.—(Hispanics of achievement)
    Includes bibliographical references (p.   ) and index.
    Summary: Examines the life and times of the Mexican general
and politician and his role in his country's politics and movement
for independence.
    ISBN 0-7910-1245-X
        0-7910-1272-7 (pbk.)
    1. Santa Anna, Antonio López de, 1794–1876. 2. Mexico—His-
tory—1821–61—Juvenile literature. 3. Presidents—Mexico—Biography—Juvenile literature. [1. Santa Anna, Antonio López de,
1794–1876. 2. Presidents—Mexico. 3. Mexico—History—1821–
61.] I. Title. II. Series.   91-37815
F1232.S232027 1992
972'.04'092—dc20   CIP
[B]   AC

Contents

Hispanics of Achievement

Oscar Arias Sánchez
Costa Rican president

Joan Baez
Mexican-American folksinger

Rubén Blades
Panamanian lawyer and entertainer

Jorge Luis Borges
Argentine writer

Juan Carlos
King of Spain

Pablo Casals
Spanish cellist and conductor

Miguel de Cervantes
Spanish writer

Cesar Chavez
Mexican-American labor leader

El Cid
Spanish military leader

Roberto Clemente
Puerto Rican baseball player

Salvador Dalí
Spanish painter

Plácido Domingo
Spanish singer

Gloria Estefan
Cuban-American singer

Gabriel García Márquez
Colombian writer

Pancho Gonzales
Mexican-American tennis player

Francisco José de Goya
Spanish painter

Frida Kahlo
Mexican painter

José Martí
Cuban revolutionary and poet

Rita Moreno
Puerto Rican singer and actress

Pablo Neruda
Chilean poet and diplomat

Antonia Novello
U.S. surgeon general

Octavio Paz
Mexican poet and critic

Javier Pérez de Cuéllar
Peruvian diplomat

Pablo Picasso
Spanish artist

Anthony Quinn
Mexican-American actor

Oscar de la Renta
Dominican fashion designer

Diego Rivera
Mexican painter

Linda Ronstadt
Mexican-American singer

Antonio López de Santa Anna
Mexican general and politician

George Santayana
Spanish philosopher and poet

Junípero Serra
Spanish missionary and explorer

Lee Trevino
Mexican-American golfer

Diego Velázquez
Spanish painter

Pancho Villa
Mexican revolutionary

CHELSEA HOUSE PUBLISHERS

INTRODUCTION

Hispanics of Achievement

Rodolfo Cardona

The Spanish language and many other elements of Spanish culture are present in the United States today and have been since the country's earliest beginnings. Some of these elements have come directly from the Iberian Peninsula; others have come indirectly, by way of Mexico, the Caribbean basin, and the countries of Central and South America.

Spanish culture has influenced America in many subtle ways, and consequently many Americans remain relatively unaware of the extent of its impact. The vast majority of them recognize the influence of Spanish culture in America, but they often do not realize the great importance and long history of that influence. This is partly because Americans have tended to judge the Hispanic influence in the United States in statistical terms rather than to look closely at the ways in which individual Hispanics have profoundly affected American culture. For this reason, it is fitting

7

that Americans obtain more than a passing acquaintance with the
origins of these Spanish cultural elements and gain an understanding of how they have been woven into the fabric of American
society.

It is well documented that Spanish seafarers were the first to
explore and colonize many of the early territories of what is today
called the United States of America. For this reason, students of
geography discover Hispanic names all over the map of the United
States. For instance, the Strait of Juan de Fuca was named after
the Spanish explorer who first navigated the waters of the Pacific
Northwest; the names of states such as Arizona (arid zone), Mon-
tana (mountain), Florida (thus named because it was reached on
Easter Sunday, which in Spanish is called the feast of Pascua
Florida), and California (named after a fictitious land in one of the
first and probably the most popular among the Spanish novels of
chivalry, *Amadis of Gaul*) are all derived from Spanish; and there
are numerous mountains, rivers, canyons, towns, and cities with
Spanish names throughout the United States.

Not only explorers but many other illustrious figures in Spanish
history have helped define American culture. For example, the
13th-century king of Spain, Alfonso X, also known as the Learned,
may be unknown to the majority of Americans, but his work on the
codification of Spanish law has greatly influenced the evolution
of American law, particularly in the jurisdictions of the Southwest.
For this contribution a statue of him stands in the rotunda of the
Capitol in Washington, D.C. Likewise, the name Diego Rivera may
be unfamiliar to most Americans, but this Mexican painter influenced many American artists whose paintings, commissioned
during the Great Depression and the New Deal era of the 1930s,
adorn the walls of government buildings throughout the United
States. In recent years the contributions of Puerto Ricans,
Mexicans, Mexican Americans (Chicanos), and Cubans in
American cities such as Boston, Chicago, Los Angeles, Miami,
Minneapolis, New York, and San Antonio have been enormous.

The importance of the Spanish language in this vast cultural complex cannot be overstated. Spanish, after all, is second only to English as the most widely spoken of Western languages within the United States as well as in the entire world. The popularity of the Spanish language in America has a long history.

In addition to Spanish exploration of the New World, the great Spanish literary tradition served as a vehicle for bringing the language and culture to America. Interest in Spanish literature in America began when English immigrants brought with them translations of Spanish masterpieces of the Golden Age. As early as 1683, private libraries in Philadelphia and Boston contained copies of the first picaresque novel, *Lazarillo de Tormes,* translations of Francisco de Quevedo's *Los Sueños,* and copies of the immortal epic of reality and illusion *Don Quixote,* by the great Spanish writer Miguel de Cervantes. It would not be surprising if Cotton Mather, the arch-Puritan, read *Don Quixote* in its original Spanish, if only to enrich his vocabulary in preparation for his writing *La fe del cristiano en 24 artículos de la Institución de Cristo, enviada a los españoles para que abran sus ojos* (The Christian's Faith in 24 Articles of the Institution of Christ, Sent to the Spaniards to Open Their Eyes), published in Boston in 1699.

Over the years, Spanish authors and their works have had a vast influence on American literature—from Washington Irving, John Steinbeck, and Ernest Hemingway in the novel to Henry Wadsworth Longfellow and Archibald MacLeish in poetry. Such important American writers as James Fenimore Cooper, Edgar Allan Poe, Walt Whitman, Mark Twain, and Herman Melville all owe a sizable debt to the Spanish literary tradition. Some writers, such as Willa Cather and Maxwell Anderson, who explored Spanish themes they came into contact with in the American Southwest and Mexico, were influenced less directly but no less profoundly.

Important contributions to a knowledge of Spanish culture in the United States were also made by many lesser known individuals—teachers, publishers, historians, entrepreneurs, and others—with a love for Spanish culture. One of the most significant of these contributions was made by Abiel Smith, a Harvard College graduate of the class of 1764, when he bequeathed stock worth $20,000 to Harvard for the support of a professor of French and Spanish. By 1819 this endowment had produced enough income to appoint a professor, and the philologist and humanist George Ticknor became the first holder of the Abiel Smith Chair, which was the very first endowed Chair at Harvard University. Other illustrious holders of the Smith Chair would include the poets Henry Wadsworth Longfellow and James Russell Lowell.

A highly respected teacher and scholar, Ticknor was also a collector of Spanish books, and as such he made a very special contribution to America's knowledge of Spanish culture. He was instrumental in amassing for Harvard libraries one of the first and most impressive collections of Spanish books in the United States. He also had a valuable personal collection of Spanish books and manuscripts, which he bequeathed to the Boston Public Library.

With the creation of the Abiel Smith Chair, Spanish language and literature courses became part of the curriculum at Harvard, which also went on to become the first American university to offer graduate studies in Romance languages. Other colleges and universities throughout the United States gradually followed Harvard's example, and today Spanish language and culture may be studied at most American institutions of higher learning.

No discussion of the Spanish influence in the United States, however brief, would be complete without a mention of the Spanish influence on art. Important American artists such as John Singer Sargent, James A. M. Whistler, Thomas Eakins, and Mary Cassatt all explored Spanish subjects and experimented with Spanish techniques. Virtually every serious American artist living today has studied the work of the Spanish masters as well as the great 20th-century Spanish painters Salvador Dalí, Joan Miró, and Pablo Picasso.

The most pervasive Spanish influence in America, however, has probably been in music. Compositions such as Leonard Bernstein's *West Side Story*, the Latinization of William Shakespeare's *Romeo and Juliet* set in New York's Puerto Rican quarter, and Aaron Copland's *Salon Mexico* are two obvious examples. In general, one can hear the influence of Latin rhythms—from tango to mambo, from guaracha to salsa—in virtually every form of American music.

This series of biographies, which Chelsea House has published under the general title HISPANICS OF ACHIEVEMENT, constitutes further recognition of—and a renewed effort to bring forth to the consciousness of America's young people—the contributions that Hispanic people have made not only in the United States but throughout the civilized world. The men and women who are featured in this series have attained a high level of accomplishment in their respective fields of endeavor and have made a permanent mark on American society.

The title of this series must be understood in its broadest possible sense: The term *Hispanics* is intended to include Spaniards, Spanish Americans, and individuals from many countries whose language and culture have either direct or indirect Spanish origins. The names of many of the people included in this series will be immediately familiar; others will be less recognizable. All, however, have attained recognition within their own countries, and often their fame has transcended their borders.

The series HISPANICS OF ACHIEVEMENT thus addresses the attainments and struggles of Hispanic people in the United States and seeks to tell the stories of individuals whose personal and professional lives in some way reflect the larger Hispanic experience. These stories are exemplary of what human beings can accomplish, often against daunting odds and by extraordinary personal sacrifice, where there is conviction and determination. Fray Junípero Serra, the 18th-century Spanish Franciscan missionary, is one such individual. Although in very poor health, he devoted the last 15 years of his life to the foundation of missions throughout California—then a mostly unsettled expanse of land—in an effort to bring a better life to Native Americans through the cultivation of crafts and animal husbandry. An example from recent times, the Mexican-American labor leader Cesar Chavez has battled bitter opposition and made untold personal sacrifices in his effort to help poor agricultural workers who have been exploited for decades on farms throughout the Southwest.

The talent with which each one of these men and women may have been endowed required dedication and hard work to develop and become fully realized. Many of them have enjoyed rewards for their efforts during their own lifetime, whereas others have died poor and unrecognized. For some it took a long time to achieve their goals, for others success came at an early age, and for still others the struggle continues. All of them, however, stand out as people whose lives have made a difference, whose achievements we need to recognize today and should continue to honor in the future.

Antonio López de Santa Anna

*Despite his father's objections, the young Antonio López de Santa Anna
was determined to pursue a military career. He became a cadet in the
Spanish army on June 10, 1810, and quickly climbed up the ranks,
becoming a lieutenant by the age of 18.*

CHAPTER 1

Royalist-Patriot

On July 16, 1829, several thousand Spanish troops landed near the tropical lowland city of Tampico, Mexico, in an effort to retake Mexico for Spain. The Spaniards anticipated little resistance from the Mexican forces because although Mexico had declared its independence from Spain eight years before, it had been unable to establish a stable central government or a strong army. The only thing that now stood between the Spanish troops and a march to Mexico City was a motley Mexican militia that was hastily recruited, poorly trained, and haphazardly armed. However, the Mexicans did have one advantage: Their leader was the renowned Antonio López de Santa Anna.

Although initially a reluctant recruit to the Mexican independence movement, Santa Anna, by 1829, was passionately committed to preventing Spain from retaking Mexico. On his own initiative, and drawing upon his authority as governor of the state of Veracruz, he had managed to recruit and arm 2,000 men. Then, at the risk of leaving the city of Veracruz, Mexico's chief seaport,

Tampico, Mexico. On July 16, 1829, Spanish troops landed on the shores of this tropical lowland city in an effort to retake the former Spanish colony. Remarkably, Santa Anna and his army of ill-equipped and poorly trained men fought off the invaders.

virtually defenseless, he chanced everything in one bold, swift thrust south. If he succeeded, he would be revered as a hero; if his army was defeated or Veracruz captured while he was in Tampico, he would be branded a fool.

The Spanish invaders were confident, well-trained, experienced, and well equipped for battle, whereas Santa Anna's troops were little more than a sorry harum-scarum rabble in arms. The two armies clashed in a series of bloody encounters from August 21 to September 10. Remarkably, Santa Anna managed to parry every move the Spanish commanders made to break out of Tampico or to defeat his men. Eventually, Santa Anna's military successes and the spread of yellow fever among the invaders combined to force the Spanish to surrender on September 11, 1829.

The moment Santa Anna learned of the Spanish surrender, he dispatched a courier to Mexico City with the news of his victory. The theater was crowded on the night Santa Anna's tired and dusty courier approached Mexican president Vicente Guerrero, who was in the audience. A hush fell over the room as he read the good news. Then, a broad smile came to the president's face, and he stood up to announce that Santa Anna's victory was complete. Ecstatic pandemonium broke out. Shouts of "Viva Santa Anna, viva

México!" echoed in the evening air, and the crowd streamed into the streets of the capital to celebrate.

Antonio López de Santa Anna was born in Jalapa, Mexico, on February 21, 1794. He grew up in the city of Veracruz, where his father, a descendant of a respected Spanish family, held an administrative position in the Spanish colonial government. His mother, Manuela Pérez de Lebrón, was also of Spanish ancestry.

Santa Anna's formal education ended early. He was not a good student and frequently quarreled with his classmates. When Santa Anna turned 14, his father obtained a job for him in a Veracruz store. His father's hope that he might channel his energy into learning a career in business was quickly dashed when the impetuous teenager derisively dismissed commercial trade work as mere "counter jumping."

Jalapa, Mexico. Santa Anna was born in this mountain village in central Mexico on February 21, 1794, but did not grow up there. While Santa Anna was a young boy, his family moved to the nearby coastal city of Veracruz, where his father took a position in the local government.

From an early age, Santa Anna had a clear vision of what course he wanted his life to take. His dream was to become a dashing cavalry officer, fiercely risking death on the frontier in the service of the Spanish crown. Santa Anna had a hard time convincing his father of the merits of a military life, but he persisted. Finally, on June 10, 1810, Santa Anna's father reluctantly secured his son an appointment as a cadet in the local infantry regiment (Regimiento Fijo de Veracruz). Nine months later, in March 1811, the new recruit enthusiastically joined the fighting against Indians on Mexico's northern frontier.

Santa Anna's military career took off like a missile. His courage in battle and willingness to endure the hardships of desert warfare so impressed his commanding officer that Santa Anna won a coveted transfer to the cavalry and then, at age 18, was promoted to first lieutenant. In 1813 he took part in the expedition that savagely crushed a premature effort by Texans to obtain independence. In one engagement, 850 rebels were trapped and slaughtered; only 93 managed to escape. More than 100 other rebels were captured and summarily shot as traitors.

While Santa Anna served in Texas, his youth and the heady power of being a cavalry officer held sway over his good judgment. He barely escaped disgrace when it was discovered that he did not possess sufficient funds to cover a gambling debt. Although he was rescued by a military colleague, the mark on his reputation and the humiliation he experienced when it was discovered that he had tried to lie his way out of the incident followed him for the rest of his life.

Still, early in 1814, Santa Anna returned to Veracruz and spent the next seven years winning recognition and promotions—to captain in 1816 and lieutenant colonel in 1821—by chasing rebels. During this period, he acquired a reputation for ruthless cunning in battle and vicious treatment of captured foes who dared to oppose him.

Like virtually all his colleagues in the army during this period, Santa Anna continued to dismiss as preposterous the idea of a successful revolt against Spanish rule. But by 1821 the long-term effects of the misguided Spanish administrative programs and the corruption of the colonial government led to such increasing popular support for Mexican independence that even military officers such as Santa Anna began to have doubts about Spain's ability to maintain control over Mexico.

Although despised by some patriots and feared by many more, Santa Anna's military prowess was considered valuable enough for the rebels to offer him the rank of full colonel. Too shrewd to let such an opportunity slip by, Santa Anna transferred his allegiance and fighting skills to the cause of independence and accepted the offer. Within a few days, he was fighting just as ferociously for independence as he had previously fought against it.

Having changed sides, Santa Anna not only had to watch out for Spanish royalists but also had to protect himself from rival rebel group leaders who would not forgive him his past. The chaos of revolution was a fertile ground for treachery, revenge, and assassination attempts, and Santa Anna was in the thick of it.

Santa Anna decided to secure his place in history as the outstanding military leader of Mexico's war of independence by liberating the city of Veracruz from Spanish control. Veracruz's defenses were considered impregnable, but this did not deter Santa Anna. On July 21, 1821, he led a vigorous assault on the city. The attack failed, but the headstrong Santa Anna was undaunted. He turned his attention to liberating other nearby cities, leaving troops at Veracruz to ensure that the Spanish did not venture outside its walls to defend other cities.

The siege of Veracruz continued until after Santa Anna returned in the fall. Then, on October 26, because of the widespread success of the rebellion in the rest of Mexico and the recognition of the need to negotiate by the Spanish viceroy, the Spanish military commander in Veracruz retreated to the harbor island fortress of San Juan de Ulúa.

Santa Anna proclaimed Veracruz liberated. Despite efforts by the independence movement leader Agustín de Iturbide to deny

In 1821, the conservative Mexican soldier and Spanish loyalist Agustín de Iturbide made a pact called the Plan of Iguala with the Mexican revolutionary Vicente Guerrero. The pact resulted in Mexican independence from Spain but also in the establishment of a monarchy. Iturbide crowned himself emperor on July 21, 1822.

him the glory of capturing the city, Santa Anna had accomplished his goal, and the people of Mexico added his name to the emerging pantheon of revolutionary heroes.

But a difficult road lay ahead for Mexico. The building of a new nation after a long colonial period can be far more difficult than winning independence. For more than three centuries, Mexico, or New Spain, as it was called, had been ruled by a highly centralized colonial administration in Spain, so it had no established laws or institutions of its own. Also, the vast majority of Mexicans were poor, illiterate Indian peasants with no real connection to any government authority beyond the hacienda owner whose land they tilled. Moreover, there was no tradition of government training or leadership experience for the descendents of Spanish settlers to build upon now that independence was achieved. And there was the added problem of hostility among diverse ethnic groups.

Iturbide realized the difficulties Mexico faced after independence and concluded, as Santa Anna and numerous other Mexican leaders eventually would, that the only hope of holding the disparate regions and elements of the nation together lay in providing a dynamic, resourceful, charismatic leader with whom the people could identify. He seized control of the national government in 1821 and then had Congress declare him the new nation's first emperor, Agustín I, on May 19, 1822.

On July 21, amid the din of artillery salvos and the clamor of innumerable marching bands, Iturbide and his family traveled in a

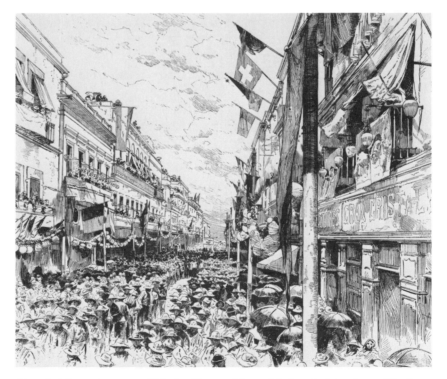

Crowds take to the streets of Mexico City to celebrate Mexican independence. The joy was short-lived, however, as Iturbide's obsessive vanity and his neglect of his duties as emperor drove the country's economy to ruin. Santa Anna, who had at first supported Iturbide, was instrumental in his ouster.

coach along a carpet of flowers to the central cathedral of Mexico City. During a high mass, he and his wife were blessed and consecrated with holy oil by the bishop of Guadalajara, and the president of Congress placed a large crown on Iturbide's head. To commemorate the event, Congress authorized a new Mexican order, the Knights of Guadalupe, to be chosen by Iturbide, who would henceforth be addressed as "His Highness."

Besides satisfying his personal vanity, Iturbide hoped that his lavish coronation would legitimize his position in the minds of the general public. He might have succeeded if he had not become so carried away with his own magnificence and indispensability that he failed to address the problems independence created. For example, the loss of Spanish trading privileges caused a sharp drop in trade that sent tax revenues plummeting. Instead of curtailing government expenditures, Iturbide increased them while granting tax breaks to win popular support. To make up the shortfall, he printed paper money. When he tried to pay the army with what quickly became worthless currency, his fate was sealed.

Iturbide managed to temporarily stifle dissent among military officers by lavishing them with promotions. He made Santa Anna a brigadier general and appointed him military commander of Jalapa and Veracruz. At first, Santa Anna supported Iturbide's rule, but as Iturbide's increasing dictatorial excesses and administrative ineffectiveness alienated the nation, Santa Anna sensed an opportunity to increase his own power at Iturbide's expense.

Aware that the young and ambitious Santa Anna was, at best, a dubious ally, Iturbide sought to eliminate him as a potential opposition leader by ordering him to report to the capital—where he could be watched or "escorted" to duty on a remote frontier posting—in December 1822. The cunning Santa Anna guessed Iturbide's plan, disobeyed his order, and dashed to Veracruz. Once inside the city's walls, he consolidated his hold over the troops stationed there and then denounced Iturbide's rule as illegal.

Santa Anna's decisive action caught Iturbide by surprise. Nevertheless, his forces mounted an attack that almost wiped out Santa Anna's army near Jalapa. Santa Anna was so disheartened after the battle that he contemplated fleeing by ship to the United States. His nerves were calmed by the reproach from fellow rebel leader Guadalupe Victoria: "You can set sail when they show you the head of Victoria." While Victoria's troops delayed Iturbide's forces, Santa Anna returned to Veracruz. He was convinced an attack was imminent and hastily prepared the defenses of the city, but the assault never materialized. Instead, other embittered generals joined Santa Anna and Victoria in rejecting Iturbide as emperor.

In February 1823 virtually all military and political leaders signed the Plan of Casa Mata. This declaration called for an end to Iturbide's effort to establish an empire, for the creation of a republic, for the election of a new national congress, and for the adoption of a new federal constitution. Faced with such overwhelming opposition, Iturbide had no choice but to accept defeat. In March, just 10 months after his coronation, he was exiled to Europe. Early the following year, Iturbide returned to Mexico, where he was captured and executed.

With Iturbide's overthrow, those who had advocated adopting a monarchist form of government were so thoroughly discredited that no one interested in securing national office dared advocate establishing an emperor again. Mexico, it was agreed, would be a republic. But virtually no one in Mexico in a position of power had any experience working within such a framework. Mexico's future looked uncertain at best.

A cypress grove near Mexico City, the Mexican capital. After Iturbide's ouster, Santa Anna proclaimed himself Protector of the Federal System. But he had no interest in the responsibilities attached to the title, and he returned to Jalapa in 1823.

CHAPTER 2

Liberal-Conservative

To the vast majority of the impoverished and illiterate Indian and mestizo peoples of Mexico, the winning of independence meant little more than the replacement of one set of oppressive government officials with another. The ancient power struggle between Peninsulars (Spanish officials from Spain) and Creoles (descendants of Spanish settlers) had simply been replaced by one between Creoles and mestizos.

Although the political situation in Mexico after independence followed class and ethnic lines much more closely than it adhered to any political agenda, there were some fairly prevalent political themes. For example, the Conservatives (supported predominantly by Creoles) advocated protecting the powers of the Catholic church, preserving the rights of the large hacienda owners, and establishing a strong central government. The Liberals advocated reducing the power of the church, establishing a balance of power between the states and the central government. Neither group would compromise its goals to coexist with the other. Thus, in order for either faction to rule, the support of the army was essential.

The army consisted of numerous groups of a few thousand men scattered around the country. Each group was much more loyal to its local commander than to the central government. The primary motivation for supporting a commander, or caudillo, was self-enrichment. When the money ran out, so did a president's military protection and thus his term of office. As Mexican governments came and went over time, one factor remained constant—no matter how many times taxes were raised or foreign loans secured, the treasury was always empty.

Although Santa Anna proclaimed himself Protector of the Federal System, he was bored by the mechanics of government— writing a constitution, formulating legislation, developing constituent support, and implementing programs—and instead of remaining in Mexico City, he returned to Jalapa in 1823. Just to be sure that he did not meddle in the writing and implementation of the new constitution, the new political leaders in Mexico City dispatched Santa Anna to quell a rebellion in the Yucatán Peninsula in 1824.

The constitution the Liberals produced in 1824 provided for Mexico to be divided into 19 states and 4 territories. Each state was empowered to elect its own governor and legislature. The national government consisted of a president, who would be elected every four years, a senate, a lower chamber of deputies, and a supreme court. The powers of the president were carefully described to discourage dictatorship. However, what the new constitution left out was more important than what it included. It did not deal with the inequitable distribution of land in Mexico, failed to provide for national public education, ignored the need for economic reform, and provided little in the way of safeguards for civil liberties.

These omissions were not a result of an effort to reach a national political consensus; the Conservatives wanted no part of this government blueprint. When the Constitution was adopted in October 1824, one conservative political leader remarked, "Today we observe [my country's] funeral." He was convinced that the new federal government, with its separation of powers and strong states, could not work in Mexico because it would weaken the national government just when strength from union was required. "We are," he continued, "like children barely out of diapers or like slaves who have just unshackled their chains. . . . We might say that nature itself has decreed our centralization."

In Mexico's first presidential election, the state legislatures chose Guadalupe Victoria as president. However, Victoria proved an ineffective leader who failed to come up with solutions to Mexico's grave economic problems or to keep his party unified.

In the first presidential election, the state legislatures chose Guadalupe Victoria as president and Nicolás Bravo as vice-president. Victoria was an honest but ineffective leader who proved incapable of dealing with the massive financial problems of the economy or of preventing the breakup of the Liberal coalition that had obtained power.

Upon his return from the Yucatán in 1825, Santa Anna did not participate in the new national government or become directly involved in national politics. Instead, he married a 14-year-old Creole girl, Ines García, spent time working on his estate, Manga de Clavo, and indulged an unusual hobby—raising fighting cocks.

Santa Anna was an imposing character. He was nearly six feet tall, whereas his countrymen were almost always considerably shorter. He was a slender man with dark eyes, a prominent nose, and light skin. People who met him were invariably struck by his energy and intensity.

In 1828, Santa Anna came out of retirement to help his old ally from the war of independence, and now president, Guadalupe Victoria, defeat a rebellion by his rival Conservative vice-president, Nicolás Bravo. The revolt failed, and Bravo and his coconspirators were sentenced to exile, but this did not settle the matter. When Manuel Gómez Pedraza, a man whom Santa Anna loathed, was elected president in 1829, the defeated rival, Vicente Guerrero, resorted to arms rather than accept defeat. Santa Anna promptly declared his support of Guerrero and started recruiting an army.

Gómez Pedraza recognized the threat Santa Anna posed. His swift dispatch of a large army caught Santa Anna by surprise. The unprepared would-be rebel leader barely managed to stave off capture long enough for a revolt by other regional commanders to save him from probable execution. Santa Anna's reward for being the first to initiate the successful revolt was another appointment as governor and commandant general of Veracruz.

On July 27, 1829, under the pretext of protecting the rights of Peninsulars whom Guerrero had expelled, Spain made its last,

Congress elected the former guerrilla fighter Vicente Guerrero as president of Mexico in 1829. However, he was overthrown and shot that same year, as the politically turbulent post-independence period in Mexico continued.

desperate bid to regain control of Mexico. An army consisting of 2,700 Spanish troops landed at Tampico. Although it was a small force, it was large enough to be a formidable military threat.

Santa Anna responded with a remarkable burst of energy. Without any assistance from the national government, he raised and equipped an army of 2,000 men in Veracruz. Forced loans from the city's merchants paid and fed the men; Santa Anna's stirring patriotic speeches recruited and inspired them.

Counting on the element of surprise, Santa Anna commandeered ships in the harbor to transport his infantry by sea to Tampico while his 600 cavalry troops traveled overland. That the

Spanish troops were divided when his forces arrived at Tampico encouraged Santa Anna to attack. He was confident that an aggressive assault would sweep him to victory. But he was wrong. Despite his personal bravery, his men were repulsed by the well-equipped Spanish troops. He had no better luck in the skirmishes that followed, but his men did manage to prevent the Spanish from escaping the disease-infested Tampico during the summer.

Finally, on September 11, with Spanish forces ravaged by illness (215 men killed in battle, 693 killed by yellow fever), the Spanish commander agreed to recognize the independence of Mexico in return for being allowed to evacuate his men to Cuba. The defeat of the Spanish invasion forces made Santa Anna a true national hero. He returned to the capital for a vast display of pomp and ceremony that culminated in Congress bestowing the title the Country's Benefactor upon him.

Santa Anna reveled in the attention, but he did not get what he truly wanted—to be appointed minister of war in the Guerrero government. Wary of the ambitious Santa Anna, Guerrero had decided not to appoint him to the powerful position. As it turned out, Guerrero could not win either way: A few months later, in 1829, Santa Anna helped lead the revolt that toppled the Guerrero government and placed his vice-president, Conservative Anastasio Bustamante, in charge.

Santa Anna supported the Conservative government and remained in retirement until Guerrero was assassinated while attempting to overthrow Bustamante. In the name of revenge, but actually because of a keen sense that it was the right time for him to make his own bid for the presidency, Santa Anna took charge of a nascent rebellion by the troops stationed in Veracruz.

Like his deceased rival Guerrero, Bustamante realized the threat Santa Anna posed and dispatched his best general to defeat

General Anastasio Bustamante served as vice-president under Guerrero but, with Santa Anna, led a revolt against Guerrero, becoming president himself in 1830. Two years later, Santa Anna drove Bustamante out of office.

him. On March 3, in a battle near the town of Tolome, Santa Anna's little army of fewer than 1,000 poorly armed men was virtually annihilated. Santa Anna, along with the few hundred men he had left, managed a hasty retreat back to Veracruz. There, as a result of the dalliance of his adversary, Santa Anna was able to organize a strong enough defense to repel a haphazard assault.

Once again fate intervened to save Santa Anna. A yellow fever epidemic forced the central government's troops to abandon their siege of the city in May. Preoccupied with rebellions in other parts of the country, Bustamante opened negotiations aimed at pacifying Santa Anna. Santa Anna cunningly used the time he obtained by pretending to bargain to rebuild his forces. After successfully defeating government troops and capturing several cities in September and October, Santa Anna began his march to the capital. He got as far as Guadalupe before Bustamante capitulated.

On December 21, 1832, Bustamante agreed to abide by the results of a new national election. Instead of staying in Mexico City and helping establish an interim federalist government, Santa Anna again returned to his hacienda with the disingenuous comment: "My whole ambition is restricted to beating my sword into a plowshare." Actually, he perceived that the best way to be overwhelmingly elected in the upcoming election was to avoid being closely identified with any faction in or out of the government. The strategy worked: 16 of the 18 state legislatures voted for him.

Santa Anna officially assumed the office of president on April 1, 1833, but he decided not to actually run the government. This task he delegated to his vice-president, the Liberal Valentín Gómez Farías.

While Santa Anna relaxed at home, Gómez Farías attempted to implement programs designed to eliminate the special privileges the church and military enjoyed. Initially, Santa Anna vigorously supported Gómez Farías's efforts. He even led armies during 1833 that defeated rebellions in the northwest and near Guanajuato. But Santa Anna was not really a Liberal, nor was he in favor of federalism. He had merely become associated with the Liberals because it had suited his goal of attaining power. Increasing protests from the church, wealthy landowners, and his military colleagues finally convinced Santa Anna in April 1834 that the goals of the Liberals were not feasible in Mexico. He concluded that what the people of Mexico really needed was the kind of strong leadership a great man, such as himself, could provide.

Characteristically, once his mind was made up, Santa Anna moved boldly and quickly. In a letter to Congress on April 16, 1834, he publicly repudiated the actions of his own vice-president. On April 24, Santa Anna arrived in Mexico City and assumed direct management of the government. He immediately dissolved Congress and suspended implementation of the Liberal legislative program. Over the course of the next eight months, he crushed several rebellions and drove Gómez Farías into exile. By December his control was complete. He used his authority to promote a strong central government and to protect the power of the church, wealthy landowners, and the military.

Santa Anna became president of Mexico on April 1, 1833. At first he trusted the running of the government to his vice-president, Valentín Gómez Farías, but Santa Anna soon became convinced that Mexico needed him to take a more active role.

CHAPTER 3

Remember the Alamo!

When the new Congress convened on January 4, 1835, Santa Anna was in a superb political position to provide effective leadership. He had a strong base of powerful Conservative support and a clear goal—to establish the supremacy of the central government in order to ensure political stability.

Although Santa Anna wanted to rule Mexico, he continued to have no interest in doing the mundane work of administering a nation. He thus placed General of Division Miguel Barragan in charge of the government as interim president and once again retired to Manga de Clavo. In addition to allowing him to relax at his estate, this arrangement enabled Santa Anna to manipulate the government without having to accept direct responsibility for its actions. This plan may have been good for Santa Anna, but it was bad for the nation.

On October 3, 1835, Barragan, with Santa Anna's concurrence, decreed that all executive power belonged to the central government, that state legislatures and town councils were to be disbanded, and that governors were to be appointed by the central government. A year later, a new constitution was adopted instituting these changes. It also provided that the Senate, rather than the state legislatures, would elect the president, who would be elected to serve an eight-year term. In addition, new property ownership qualifications were imposed that excluded all but the very wealthy from serving in the national legislature.

In effect, everything the liberal Constitution of 1824 had promised, the conservative Constitution of 1836 contradicted. Santa Anna's decision to abolish the federal republic and to replace it with a strong centralist state precipitated a series of interrelated events that were to dominate his life and his country for the next 12 years. Liberal politicians in Mexico were dismayed, and several led revolts against him. Santa Anna dealt swiftly and successfully with the first state government's refusal to accept the new political order. On May 11, 1835, he soundly defeated a rebel army near Guadalupe. But the most serious opposition by far came from the northern province of Texas. His actions to suppress rebellion there eventually culminated in a disastrous war with the United States.

In 1835, Mexico stretched from the Yucatán in the south to Oregon, Colorado, and Texas in the north. California was sparsely settled and controlled largely by a network of mission settlements. The huge province of Texas was another matter. American settlers had been coming to the province since the late 18th century. Spain had actually encouraged the settlers in the early 19th century in the hope of creating a buffer zone between its territories and the rapidly expanding United States. Mexico had also encouraged immigrant settlement during the 1820s, but its efforts to bring the geographically remote and ethnically diverse province under tighter control failed and served only to increase demands by Texans for local autonomy. The highly centralized structure of the new Conservative government in Mexico was anathema to Texans.

On November 3, 1835, the government of Texas declared the province independent. Santa Anna interpreted the actions of the

Texans as traitorous, and he rushed to San Luis Potosí, where he raised and equipped an army of 6,000 men. He explained in his memoirs, "As chief executive of the goverment . . . I declared that I would maintain the territorial integrity of my country whatever the cost. . . . Stimulated by . . . courageous feelings I took command of the campaign myself, preferring the uncertainties of the war to the easy and much coveted life of the palace." His plan was to crush the rebellion with a single, decisive military stroke.

On January 2, 1836, he led his virtually untrained and poorly equipped army on a two-month winter trek through harsh desert weather to San Antonio. Speed was so essential to him that he left his heavy artillery in San Luis Potosí along with his supply wagons. His confidence that his troops could live off the land proved ill founded, and many of his men died and deserted; but the bulk of his army survived intact. Its arrival succeeded in catching the Texans unprepared, enabling Santa Anna to strike before the local militia could be formed into a credible fighting force.

Santa Anna encountered his first organized resistance in San Antonio. It was not what he expected or wanted. Instead of confronting rebel leader Sam Houston at the head of the main body of the rebel army, he found a hastily fortified former Franciscan mission named the Alamo. Houston ordered the 183 men at the Alamo to relinquish control of the mission before they were surrounded and to join his forces in a strategic retreat. The commander of the Alamo, William B. Travis, refused to obey the order. When he gave his fellow defenders (including the renowned Indian-fighter Davy Crockett and the former slave-trader Jim Bowie) the right to leave if they wished, they voted to stay and fight. For several days prior to March 6, 1836, Santa Anna laid siege to the Alamo. Without his heavy artillery, the only way to take the mission was by frontal assault. Santa Anna decided to deal with the Alamo's defenders the same way he had seen Texas rebels dealt with 20 years before as a young man: He ordered their annihilation. Late on the afternoon of March 5, the Texans might have heard, but

Santa Anna

Dawn at the Alamo by the 19th-century Irish-American painter Henry Arthur McArdle. When the province of Texas declared its independence from Mexico in November 1835, Santa Anna moved swiftly to quell the rebellion. At the Alamo, a Franciscan mission in San Antonio, a critical battle took place in which Santa Anna's troops routed the rebel forces.

would not have understood, the significance of the sounds made by a single bugle. It was the *degüello*, a battle call used since the time of the Spanish wars against the Moors to signal that the engagement to follow was to be to the death—no prisoners would be taken.

On the morning of March 6, during the course of a battle that lasted a little more than an hour, Santa Anna's men successfully stormed the Alamo, despite having only half the number of cannon as had the Alamo defenders and despite having rifles with much shorter range. Although Mexican casualties numbered in the hundreds, the walls of the Alamo were breeched in numerous places after several assaults, and the fighting continued inside the mission. Eventually, nearly all the 183 men in the mission were killed. Crockett and six other defenders surrendered and were later executed. One man, Louis Rose, escaped, and three women, two children, and a black servant boy were spared.

After the assault on the Alamo, small rebel guerrilla bands appeared to be all that was left to fight. With the hope of quickly wrapping up the campaign, Santa Anna divided his forces into four groups. While he dallied in San Antonio, enjoying the company of a new teenage mistress, one division, under the command of General José Urrea, captured 365 rebels near Goliad. The Texans thought that by surrendering they could escape the fate of the men at the Alamo. They were wrong. On the grounds that he had been ordered by the central government to treat foreign-born rebels as pirates and Mexican rebels as traitors, Santa Anna ordered their execution. When his command was questioned, Santa Anna reiterated his order in writing on March 23, ending his message, "I trust that, in reply to this, you will inform me that public vengeance has been satisfied by the punishment of such detestable delinquents." Only a handful of the unarmed men, hiding in bushes, managed to escape the carnage that came at daybreak on March 27.

The Goliad and Alamo atrocities failed to achieve Santa Anna's political goals. Instead of terrorizing the Texans into submission, the cries of "Remember the Alamo!" and "Remember Goliad!" unified and invigorated the faltering rebel movement. Supplies and men from the United States began to pour into Texas.

Less than a month after the Goliad massacre, Sam Houston's strategy of dividing and exhausting the Mexican troops achieved dramatic success. On April 21, while Santa Anna and most of his 1,100 weary men stationed in San Jacinto were sleeping, the Texas army of 800 men, led by Houston, launched a devastating surprise attack. Caught completely off guard, the groggy Santa Anna emerged from his tent, panicked, screamed that the battle was lost, mounted a horse, and fled. Within 30 minutes, half his men were killed and the rest were either wounded or captured. As for Santa Anna, he did not manage to get very far; he was picked up by an American patrol, identified, and brought to Houston.

By the time he met with Sam Houston, Santa Anna had regained his composure. Houston was careful to ensure Santa Anna's safety; as a bargaining tool for gaining recognition of Texas independence, the Mexican was worth much more alive than dead. Almost immediately, negotiations began, and on May 14, 1836, Santa Anna made numerous concessions and even signed a secret treaty.

In return for the promise of his release, Santa Anna agreed to order the end of all hostilities, the exchange of prisoners, the withdrawal of his forces from Texas, and the restoration of all seized private property. He also pledged never to take up arms against the people of Texas again. In the secret treaty, he agreed to work to persuade the central government to recognize the independence of Texas with the Rio Grande as its southern boundary.

Santa Anna was scheduled to sail from Velasco to Veracruz on June 1. In fact, he was already on board the *Invincible* when popular

42

A McArdle painting of the Battle of San Jacinto. In April 1836, a Texas army of 800 men surprised and routed Santa Anna's troops while they were sleeping at their camp in San Jacinto. The Texans rallied to the cries of "Remember the Alamo!"

Surrender of Santa Anna *by the 19th-century American artist William Henry Huddle. At San Jacinto, Santa Anna quickly mounted his horse and attempted to escape, but the Texan onslaught overwhelmed him and his men. He was captured and brought to General Sam Houston, leader of the Texas army.*

sentiment against his release led to his forced return to shore. Afraid that the screaming mob demanding vengeance for Goliad would tear him to pieces, Santa Anna begged the captain of the vessel to set sail, but the man refused. Miraculously, the efficient military escort managed to get him to a jail cell.

It is likely that Santa Anna would have been assassinated or lynched soon after his incarceration except for the intervention of Stephen F. Austin. Santa Anna had released Austin from prison once in Mexico City. Austin's suggestion that Santa Anna write to President Andrew Jackson, a highly esteemed figure among the Texans, bought enough time for tempers to cool. In the letter Santa Anna mailed to Jackson on July 4, he asked Jackson to intervene to

A political cartoon from the period depicts Santa Anna (center) surrendering his sword to Sam Houston. To save his own skin, Santa Anna made numerous concessions to the Texan, including a promise to try to persuade the Mexican government to recognize the Rio Grande as the southern boundary of an independent Texas.

In addition to the many promises he made to Sam Houston, Santa Anna gave him this ornate snuff box. Although Houston had spared Santa Anna's life, many sought revenge for the Alamo massacre, and Santa Anna, once released from prison, had to be accompanied by an armed guard.

enforce the provisions of the treaties he had signed. Although Jackson's reply, delivered early in October, offered Santa Anna no help, the U.S. president's letter gave Santa Anna the pretext he needed to go to Washington, D.C.

On November 25, under guard, Santa Anna began a long journey across the United States. He arrived in Washington, D.C., on January 18, 1837, with two stated objectives: to convince his allies in Texas that he was fervently on their side and to assess President Jackson's attitude toward an independent Texas. During a brief meeting at the White House, Jackson made it clear that he would not become involved in undermining the independence of Texas. He pointed out that the Mexican government had disassociated itself from any agreements Santa Anna had or might make

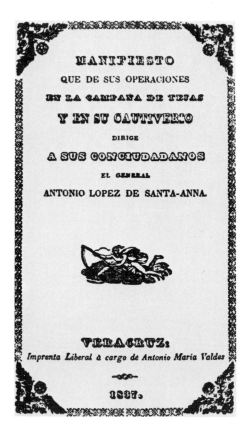

In November 1836, Santa Anna traveled to Washington, D.C., to meet with U.S. president Andrew Jackson, who was critical of the Mexican general's conduct in the war with Texas. Santa Anna attempted to answer Jackson's accusations, and a year later he issued this manifesto to further defend his actions.

while in captivity. He also asked Santa Anna about the Alamo and Goliad massacres. Santa Anna replied that he accepted Texan independence and repeated his claim that he was only following orders at the Alamo and Goliad. Jackson, who was convinced that Santa Anna would regain the presidency upon his return to Mexico, was evidently satisfied with the result of their discussion. He invited Santa Anna to dinner and authorized his transport to Veracruz by the U.S. Navy.

Humiliated and discredited, Santa Anna, now considered a traitor, arrived in Veracruz on February 21, 1837. The reception he received was so hostile that for his safety he was given an American escort to his home. Once back at Manga de Clavo, Santa Anna tried to defend his actions in Texas. He did nothing in the name of the nation, he argued. The promises he made as an individual, to secure his release, were not binding on the government. Where, he asked, was the treason? But in his heart he knew better. He confided to a friend, "The end of my public career has arrived."

It certainly seemed that the hero of Tampico had been forgotten. The ballot results for president that year were Bustamante, 57 votes, Santa Anna, 2 votes.

Upon his return from the United States, Santa Anna retired to his Manga de Clavo hacienda. But he would not remain out of the spotlight for long: Less than 18 months after his return, Santa Anna was called on to help defend the city of Veracruz against the French.

CHAPTER 4

Dictator

Santa Anna was not destined to live in quiet retirement at Manga de Clavo for long. Less than 18 months after his return from the United States in disgrace, a valiant attempt to defend Veracruz from foreign military occupation returned him to the status of a national hero.

In early 1838, King Louis Philippe of France demanded that Mexico pay the French government 600,000 pesos. The money was to be used to compensate French citizens for property they had lost in Mexico during the political chaos that had engulfed the nation since the war of independence. Among the French claims were those of a pastry cook whose store had been ransacked by Mexican soldiers in 1828. This claim was seized upon by journalists at the time to give a name—the Pastry War—to the fighting that broke out between the two nations after the French fleet blockaded Veracruz harbor in April 1838.

Mexico had no navy to oppose the French blockade. To prevent the French from occupying the port through which the Mexican

Santa Anna and the Mexican general Manuel Rincón determined that the island for-
tress of San Juan de Ulúa could not be defended and so surrendered it to the French.
The decision angered President Bustamante, but Rincón, not Santa Anna, was
blamed, and Bustamante appointed the latter commander of the forces at Veracruz.

government received most of its tariff (import tax) revenue, President Bustamante dispatched General Manuel Rincón to implement defensive measures. Shortly after his arrival in Veracruz, a
French naval artillery barrage demonstrated just how obsolete
Mexico's coastal fortifications were by demolishing several sec-
tions of the moss-mottled walls surrounding the island fortress of
San Juan de Ulúa.

Santa Anna believed the real goal of the French government's
action was the occupation of Mexico. He was convinced that Louis
Philippe wanted to crown a French nobleman emperor of Mexico.
On his own initiative he traveled to Veracruz and offered his
assistance to Rincón. Rincón accepted Santa Anna's help and asked
him to assess the possibility of defending San Juan de Ulúa.

Following a quick inspection, Santa Anna reported that the lack of ammunition, the shortage of properly trained troops, and the inability of the 16th-century walls of the island fortress to withstand 19th-century artillery bombardment dictated the necessity of abandoning the fort. Rincón agreed.

After the fortress was given up on November 28, Rincón agreed on behalf of the Mexican government to provide the money France demanded in order to avoid a bombardment and occupation of the city. Since the crisis appeared settled, Santa Anna returned to Manga de Clavo.

The decision to abandon San Juan de Ulúa enraged Bustamante and Congress. Because Rincón had not mentioned Santa

Santa Anna lost most of his left leg below the knee in battle against the French at Veracruz. In his report to the government, he intimated that he was on his deathbed, garnering considerable sympathy from the Mexican people, who soon returned to him the status of national hero.

Anna's support for surrendering the fort and negotiating a settlement, the full blame for the disaster was placed upon Rincón. On December 1, rather than pay the damages Louis Philippe demanded, Mexico officially declared war on France.

Once it was decided to go to war, Bustamante and Congress concluded that there was only one man in Mexico who could organize an effective defense against the now widely anticipated French invasion—the hero of Tampico, Santa Anna.

As soon as Santa Anna learned of his appointment as commander of the military forces at Veracruz, he hastened back to the city. On December 3 and late into the night of December 4, he worked on developing a plan to defend the city. Finally, exhausted, he went to bed only to be awakened just before dawn by the sound of gunfire. Several thousand French troops were advancing on Veracruz.

Santa Anna leaped from his bed and dashed from the building while still in his bedclothes. His disheveled condition caused several French soldiers to mistake Santa Anna for a butler and let him escape to safety. His second in command, who wasted precious seconds putting on his clothes, was captured along with his aide.

The humiliated hero of Tampico recovered his composure, put on his clothes, and then rallied the Mexican troops within the city to resist the French attack. Then, driven by the need to redeem his honor, he attempted to rout the French as they withdrew to their ships. In an impulsive display of bravery, he mounted a horse and personally led a charge toward the dock where the French troops were reembarking.

Anticipating the need for a defense against just such a charge, the French had hidden a strategically placed cannon loaded with shrapnel. The French gunners calmly waited until the galloping Santa Anna came into range and then fired. The blast shot Santa Anna's horse out from under him and virtually tore his left foot off. The Mexican offensive crumbled along with Santa Anna, and the French completed their withdrawal.

Santa Anna's cork leg. Soon after he returned to Manga de Clavo to recover from his battle wound, Santa Anna was called on to serve as interim president while Busta-mante led troops into battle. Later, Santa Anna also returned to the battlefield, directing his troops from a litter.

Santa Anna's left foot was so shattered that it and a portion of his leg below the knee had to be amputated. A few hours before the operation, Santa Anna composed a report to the government in which he claimed that he and his men had driven the enemy back into their boats at the point of the bayonet: "We conquered, yes, we conquered: Mexican arms secured a glorious victory in the plaza; and the flag of Mexico remained triumphant: I was wounded in this last effort and probably this will be the last victory that I shall offer my native land." Dramatically anticipating death, he then asked the people of Mexico not to deny him "the only title I wish to leave my children: that of a 'good' Mexican."

A Mexican battle flag captured by the Texans at San Jacinto. Santa Anna's reputation as a general, marred by his defeat at San Jacinto, was rejuvenated by his heroics at Veracruz. Likewise, his political career was revitalized when he assumed the presidency in Bustamante's absence.

When news of his deathbed request was read, the tears of a grateful nation washed away the disgrace of San Jacinto. Santa Anna had not only regained his status as a national hero, he had become a martyr. British mediation resolved the French dispute the following spring. In return for the promise of the Mexican government to pay the demanded 600,000 pesos over a period of years, the French blockade was lifted.

While Santa Anna returned to Manga de Clavo to recover from his wounds under the expert care of his wife, the political situation in Mexico deteriorated. Federalist uprisings increased during the early months of 1839. To show his support, Santa Anna agreed to travel to Mexico City in February to serve as interim president while Bustamante defeated the main rebel army.

When Bustamante proved unable to locate the rebel force, Santa Anna set out on his own a few months later. On May 3, while still being carried in a litter, he directed a battle in which his forces of some 2,000 men virtually wiped out the rebel army and its leaders. The fighting was so savage that when Santa Anna gave the captured rebel leaders three hours to settle their personal affairs before their execution, one of them replied that if he had captured Santa Anna, he would have given him only three minutes.

The triumphant return of Santa Anna to Mexico City was accompanied by a huge display of public support. Church bells rang, and thousands of the city's inhabitants turned out to cheer him. The presidency was his for the taking, but rather than challenge Bustamante for power, Santa Anna shrewdly returned to Manga de Clavo. He knew that he could topple Bustamante and that Bustamante knew it. The issue was simply a matter of timing. After leading troops to preserve Bustamante's administration one more time in July 1840, Santa Anna decided in the late summer of 1841 that the time had come for him to take charge. Once Santa Anna's opposition became publicly known, Bustamante's presidency was over.

The chaos that followed the toppling of Bustamante provided Santa Anna with the opportunity he needed that fall to reascend to the presidency. On October 6, Bustamante formally accepted an agreement that arranged for Santa Anna to be "elected" his successor. Santa Anna took the oath of office on October 10, 1841, beginning the longest uninterrupted period—three years—that he would ever serve as president. Although he accomplished some public urban renewal projects in Mexico City, maintained cordial relations with the United States despite the continuing unresolved issue of Texan independence, and authorized railroad construction, his regime is recalled chiefly for its degeneration into a despotism on a scale matched previously only by Iturbide.

Shortly after he assumed the presidency, Santa Anna began establishing a military dictatorship. He gradually concentrated power in himself and increasingly disregarded the decisions of

Congress. In 1843 he orchestrated the adoption of a new constitution, Las Bases Orgánicas, which required a person to have tremendous wealth in order to be eligible to serve in Congress and guaranteed complete protection of the special privileges of the military and the church.

Styling himself as the Napoléon of the West, Santa Anna insisted on huge cavalry escorts, great public celebrations on his name day, and the erection of bronze and marble statues of himself in public squares and buildings throughout Mexico City. Then, his self-obsession knowing no bounds, he had the amputated portion of his left leg dug up and carried in a great procession through the streets of Mexico City to the cemetery of Santa Paula, where it was placed, after a long and solemn ceremony, in an urn atop a stone column.

Santa Anna retired to this hacienda near Jalapa for a period following his wife's death in 1844. That same year, the 50-year-old Santa Anna announced his engagement to a 15-year-old girl, María Dolores de Tosta, undermining his own reputation.

In 1842, Santa Anna had invested a huge sum in the purchase of a hacienda named El Encero in the highlands east of Jalapa. The hacienda was located in a much healthier climate than Manga de Clavo, but this did not save Ines García de Santa Anna, who died of pneumonia after a long illness, on August 23, 1844. Although his wife was deeply loved by the people of Mexico and had borne him five children, Santa Anna had for some time lost interest in her. He appreciated her efficient management of Manga de Clavo, but he had never made any effort to hide his penchant for beautiful young mistresses. She had endured his unfaithfulness and erratic political career faithfully and without complaint.

Following his wife's death, Santa Anna retired to his hacienda, ostensibly to cope with his emotional devastation. Then, the 50-year-old Santa Anna stunned the nation by announcing his decision to marry a 15-year-old girl named María Dolores de Tosta, on October 3, 1844. Santa Anna's failure to wait for the traditional period of mourning before remarrying offended the many admirers of his deceased first wife and seriously undermined public support for his presidency at a crucial time.

Santa Anna's popularity continued to decline rapidly in the fall of 1844 as a result of the deteriorating financial condition of the country. Although he had accomplished a dramatic increase in government revenues by implementing numerous new taxes and increasing tariff duties, Santa Anna had actually increased the national deficit through massive government spending aimed at pacifying the army and rewarding his supporters with outlandishly profitable contracts.

When Santa Anna's ingenious methods of obtaining money through forced domestic loans and foreign credit finally ran out, his allies as well as his enemies quickly moved to topple his regime. On October 30, 1844, his cohort in the 1841 rebellion, General Mariano Paredes, denounced him. When Paredes advanced on

Mexico City in November with his army, Santa Anna found himself unable to obtain enough funding to field a force to defeat the invaders. On December 2, 1844, just a few days after Santa Anna fled to the city of Querétaro, Congress formally declared his dictatorial conduct as president unacceptable. His presidency was officially over. News of his downfall prompted mobs to roam the city toppling his statues. One angry group retrieved his severed leg, dragged it through the streets of the capital, and then burned and pulverized it into dust.

After an unsuccessful, desperate effort to negotiate safe passage to exile in early January 1845, Santa Anna realized it was time to flee for his life. To avoid attracting attention, he and a few loyal followers exchanged their military uniforms for those of muleteers and proceeded to make their way with a mule train to Jalapa.

The ruse did not work. On the night of January 14, 1845, a group of Indians ambushed the party. His compatriots escaped by dashing into the forest, but Santa Anna could not because of his wooden leg. Once the Indians realized who they had unwittingly captured, they decided to secure vengeance rather than a reward. A huge pot was filled with water, banana leaves, and chilies. Their plan to boil Santa Anna alive, wrap him in banana leaves, and then present him to the authorities as a kind of huge, well-spiced tamale was only prevented by the intervention of the village priest.

The next day, a relieved Santa Anna was turned over to the regular government forces and imprisoned at Jalapa. In a letter to the minister of war protesting his treatment, he said, "My situation is worse than when I was a prisoner of war among the Texan soldiers of fortune." Santa Anna remained incarcerated at Jalapa while testimony was taken against him in Mexico City. He was indicted for treason, but no political leader in Mexico wanted to be responsible for authorizing his trial and execution. Instead, during the next few months there was a lengthy public examination of his conduct while in office. Once tempers had cooled, Santa Anna's political opponents concluded that the real question was not whether Santa Anna was guilty of any crime but what the political situation in the country indicated should be done with him.

On May 24, Santa Anna was offered a deal: The indictment would be dropped; he would be allowed to keep his three properties—El Enccro (88,000 acres), Manga de Clavo (220,000 acres), and Paso de Varas (175,000 acres); and he would be granted a stipend equal to half the pay of a general if he agreed to renounce all claims to the presidency and accept exile to Venezuela. Because the most likely alternative was execution, Santa Anna accepted.

On June 3, 1845, at Antigua, near Veracruz, Santa Anna and his bride (who only a few months before had visions of becoming the queen of Mexico), along with other members of his household and family, left Mexico. Before his vessel set sail, however, Santa Anna pleaded for sympathy and understanding from his countrymen:

> Mexicans! In my old age and mutilated, surrounded by a
> wife and innocent children, I am going into exile to seek a
> resting place among strangers. Mercifully forgive the mis-
> takes I made unintentionally; and believe me, in God's
> name, that I have labored sincerely that you should be inde-
> pendent, free, and happy.

Santa Anna in formal military garb. In exile in Cuba in 1845, Santa Anna watched from afar the unfolding of events in Mexico, which was shaken by serious economic decline and political instability. In little more than a year after Santa Anna's exile, the presidency changed hands three times.

CHAPTER 5

The Mexican-American War

From Havana, Cuba, Santa Anna continued to monitor events in Mexico. He watched as Mariano Paredes, the man who had led the revolt that ousted him, proceeded to topple the government of his replacement, José Joaquín Herrera, in December 1845. The ostensible reason for Paredes's action this time was the rumor that Herrera had begun negotiations with a special envoy of the United States, John Slidell, to recognize the independence of Texas.

On January 2, 1846, Paredes became president himself. But he was no more successful than Herrera in coping with the collapse of the economy, the inability to obtain foreign loans, suppressing rebellions, and negotiating a solution to the annexation of Texas by the United States on March 1, 1845. The inability of Paredes to obtain funds to pay the army along with the outbreak of war between Mexico and the United States in May 1846 led to the overthrow of the government on August 6.

Havana, Cuba. Santa Anna's exile in Cuba was brief. When President Valentín Gómez Farías invited him to return to Mexico to lead its armed forces in a war with the United States, Santa Anna accepted. Meanwhile, he was secretly looking to strike a deal with U.S. envoys.

The third man to control Mexico within slightly more than a year of Santa Anna's exile was the Liberal political leader Valentín Gómez Farías, who assumed control of a politically unstable nation at war and with no money. Only one man had a history of being able to defend Mexico's independence in such circumstances—Santa Anna. Gómez Farías knew Santa Anna could not be trusted, but he felt he had no choice but to invite him back to assume command of Mexico's defense. Santa Anna assured Gómez Farías that he had no political ambitions, that all he wanted to do was to lead the effort to protect Mexico and then quietly retire to his El Encero hacienda.

While he was making promises to Gómez Farías, Santa Anna was secretly negotiating with envoys from the United States in Cuba. He told them that if he was allowed to pass through the U.S.

Valentín Gómez Farías, who had served as Santa Anna's vice-president, became president himself in 1846. After introducing numerous social and economic reforms in Mexico, he was ousted by Santa Anna that same year.

blockade at Veracruz, he would do everything he could to end the war along the terms sought by the United States—recognition of the Rio Grande as the southern boundary of Texas and the purchase of California. Santa Anna even outlined a strategy to the U.S. envoy for defeating Mexico that was very similar to the one actually employed.

U.S. president James K. Polk did not trust Santa Anna any more than Gómez Farías did, but he decided that a weakened Santa Anna at the head of a functioning Mexican government was preferable to chaos. On May 13, 1846, the commander of the U.S. fleet patrolling Mexican waters received his orders: "If Santa Anna endeavors to enter the Mexican ports, you will allow him to pass freely."

On August 16, 1846, just 1 year, 2 months, and 13 days after he had left Veracruz in disgrace, Santa Anna returned to accept command of Mexico's military forces. Ironically, the United States had assisted in the return to the presidency of Mexico the one man capable of organizing and leading an effective national resistance campaign against it.

Santa Anna's strategy for repelling the American attack was simple: defeat the invasion force of General Zachary Taylor in northern Mexico and then counter an expected U.S. landing at Veracruz. To accomplish this task, he forced the church to make a huge loan; recruited and organized an army of 20,000 men at San Luis Potosí; and then, with only minimal training and supplies, marched that army north across the desert during a harsh winter storm to confront Taylor at the Battle of Buena Vista.

The Battle of Buena Vista. In 1847, Santa Anna bravely led his troops into battle at Buena Vista, where he displayed courage and shrewd tactical efforts. However, despite the Mexican general's well-conceived battle plan, the U.S. forces proved too powerful for the Mexican army.

Santa Anna's performance at Buena Vista marked the pinnacle of his military career. Although his army of 13,000 men outnumbered Taylor's, the U.S. troops were much better equipped, had ample artillery support, and abundant medical and food supplies.

During the two days of the battle, February 22 and 23, 1847, Santa Anna, wearing a white duster and an old straw hat, rode along the Mexican front lines, personally encouraging and directing his men. Even the U.S. soldiers marveled at his bravery. When his horse was shot out from under him, Santa Anna immediately mounted another and continued to lead his men into battle.

Bravery and a well-executed battle plan were not enough, however, to achieve victory. The Mexican army had suffered a far greater number of casualties than had the U.S. forces, and it had almost run out of food and water. When told by his officers on the night of February 23 that his men were so exhausted that a U.S. offensive the next day could result in a rout, Santa Anna decided to withdraw his troops from the battlefield.

As the Mexican army marched back to San Luis Potosí, Santa Anna shrewdly snatched victory from defeat by racing ahead of his army to Mexico City with two American flags captured during the fighting and proclaiming that a glorious victory had been achieved. But when he arrived in Mexico City, Santa Anna found yet another rebellion. This time it was not against his leadership but that of Gómez Farías, the man he had left in charge as chief executive and whose new liberal reforms had threatened the special privileges of the church. On March 31, encouraged by a gift of two million pesos from the church, Santa Anna once again repealed all the reforms instituted by Gómez Farías and sent him into exile.

In early April, with his presidency firmly secured, Santa Anna turned his attention to coping with the invading army of General Winfield Scott, from Veracruz. Once again, he was able to recruit and organize an army in a short amount of time, but his men were poorly equipped and inadequately trained, and he lacked a carefully conceived battle strategy. Consequently, on April 18 he was defeated at the Battle of Cerro Gordo.

The fate of the army at Cerro Gordo might have been different if the arrogant Santa Anna had listened to the warnings of his engineers. They correctly pointed out that two areas Santa Anna did not fortify—a steep hill and woodland ravine—could be used to outflank the army. Santa Anna dismissed their concerns with the scathing remark "cowards never feel safe anyway." During the battle, just as his subordinate officers had predicted, the U.S. soldiers placed artillery on the hilltop with devastating effect and then outflanked the Mexican troops by cutting a path through the ravine. The rout was so complete that to escape capture, Santa Anna was forced to flee without both his extra wooden leg and a chest containing 50,000 pesos.

The militarily defeated and psychologically devastated Santa Anna returned to Mexico City. Whether he actually became secretly involved in trying to arrange a Mexican capitulation at this time is uncertain. He may have just been trying to buy time, or he may have actually accepted that defeat was inevitable. In June, through secret couriers, Santa Anna proposed to General Scott and State Department official Nicholas Trist that the U.S. forces should march on Mexico City, capture the outlying posts near the capital, and then halt until he could convince the Mexican Congress to accept the necessity of negotiating a peace treaty. On June 12, Scott gave $10,000 to Trist to pass along to Santa Anna's agents. It was evidently the first of a number of large sums provided to Santa Anna to ensure his cooperation in the upcoming campaign. He was ostensibly using the money to bribe Mexican legislators to agree to sue for peace.

On August 7, Scott began his advance over the mountains to Mexico City. None of the narrow passes that might have impeded his march were blocked or defended. Whether this was a result of deceit or part of Santa Anna's plan of letting Scott penetrate into the valley of Mexico so that he could then cut his supply lines and

Mexico City. As U.S. forces under the command of General Winfield Scott advanced on the city, Santa Anna did what he could to strengthen its fortifications. But his efforts were to no avail; Mexico City was captured on September 14, 1847.

prevent his reinforcement or retreat will never be known. The plan he had communicated to Scott that he was prepared to follow was very close to what he actually did. He had his men make a token effort to halt the advance of the U.S. forces and then pulled them back behind El Peñón fortified hill south of Mexico City. Surely, he reasoned to Scott, with the U.S. troops in sight the Mexican Congress would see the need to settle the war. Perhaps he really meant it when he wrote such sentiments to Scott, but the hostility of the population in the valley of Mexico to any suggestion of capitulation forced him to do his best to defeat Scott.

While General Scott slowly advanced his army toward Mexico City, Santa Anna worked furiously to raise one of his own. His efforts were undermined in disputes with rival generals, especially Gabriel Valencia, and Congress, but he persevered. He did not want Mexico humiliated. In his heart Santa Anna always wanted to fight and defeat the United States, but he knew he lacked the military capacity needed to achieve victory.

When Scott's army arrived on August 20, Santa Anna, who remained at the strategically located fortification on El Peñón, ordered the men at Contreras and Churubusco to fall back behind the well-fortified defensive line he had constructed after they had briefly engaged the U.S. troops. This time Santa Anna had a well-thought-out and properly conceived overall defensive battle plan. The only problem was that he had not counted on the refusal of General Valencia to obey the order to retreat.

Valencia's army fought heroically, but as Santa Anna had anticipated, his troops were still eventually overwhelmed. Under the burden of the calamity caused by the annihilation of Valencia's army, Santa Anna's whole strategy collapsed. Without the men from Contreras and Churubusco to cover the flank of his dug-in troops on top of El Peñón, his position became untenable. The Mexican army was forced to abandon most of the artillery it possessed in order to scramble into Mexico City. The dignity Santa Anna hoped to preserve for Mexico and the strong bargaining position a powerful defense might have offered while negotiating with the Americans was lost.

The loss of one-third of his army in one day gave Santa Anna no choice but to open negotiations, if not surrender, in order to at least buy time to construct hasty defensive positions in the city. The catastrophe of August 20 and the presence of U.S. forces outside the city did not achieve the results Scott desired. The resolve of the Mexican Congress and the people of the city seemed to only stiffen.

In a burst of energy, Santa Anna did everything possible to fortify strategic positions in the city with the few remaining troops he had under his command. Because he knew the U.S. troops would prevail, he also developed a contingency plan: Once the city was captured, the Mexican army would resort to guerrilla tactics.

But it was too late for Mexico and for Santa Anna. He had lost too many battles and was widely suspected of having betrayed the nation in his now widely suspected secret dealings with the United States. While Santa Anna was busy organizing troops in Mexico City, General Valencia launched a rebellion in Toluca on August 25 with two goals: fighting the American army to the death and beheading Santa Anna.

On September 8 the U.S. forces took Molino del Rey and then advanced on the last Mexican stronghold, at Chapultepec. The defenders of Chapultepec included teenage cadets. When the fort was about to fall, the teenagers committed suicide by hurling themselves from Chapultepec's high walls. Although Santa Anna did not appear at Molino del Rey or Chapultepec, he relentlessly drove his men and officers. Nevertheless, Mexico City was captured on September 14, 1847.

With the capital and the country occupied by U.S. forces, the Mexican Congress appointed a new president and finally began the negotiations that culminated in the signing of the Treaty of Guadalupe Hidalgo on February 2, 1848. Under its terms, Mexico received $15,000,000 and the cancellation of all outstanding claims. The United States got Mexican recognition of its annexation of Texas and ownership of the territory that is now California, New Mexico, Arizona, Nevada, Utah, and part of Colorado—about half of Mexico's national domain.

After fleeing to Puebla and then barely escaping capture by a group of Texas Rangers bent on revenge, Santa Anna briefly became a guerrilla resistance leader before being ordered by the new national government to surrender his command to his old rival General Manuel Rincón. He was also ordered to report for a court-martial to consider his military conduct during the war. The deeply depressed and embittered Santa Anna spent the next six months as a fugitive in his own country before finally accepting defeat. On April 5, 1848, he embarked from Antigua once again, this time for exile in Jamaica.

Kingston, Jamaica. Once more exiled from Mexico, Santa Anna spent two years in Jamaica, but he found the island's cultural norms unsettling. Consequently, he, his family, and his entourage moved to Colombia in April 1850.

CHAPTER 6

His Most Serene Highness

Santa Anna spent his first two years in exile in Jamaica, where he and his retinue of family and friends lived well, apparently on money he had placed in safekeeping abroad while president. But the British-controlled island proved unsatisfactory as a long-term residence. The isolation caused by his never having learned to speak English and the disorienting effects of British cultural norms led Santa Anna to move to Cartagena, Colombia, in April 1850.

In Colombia, Santa Anna purchased a large hacienda in Turbaco. For the next several years, he lived the life of a wealthy country gentleman. In addition to managing his hacienda and indulging his passion for cockfighting, he won considerable local public esteem among Colombian Conservatives by financing the rebuilding of numerous village churches.

During Santa Anna's exile, the contempt of Mexicans for his failures and shortcomings in the war against the United States melted away. Compared with the chaos that had followed his departure—five Liberal presidents from 1848 to 1853 proved incapable

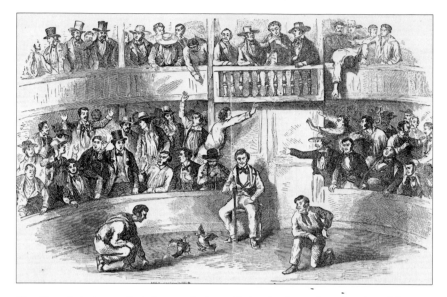

Gamblers despair over their losses, gloat over their winnings, cheer, howl, and bet furiously as two frantic birds gouge and bloody each other in a Havana cockpit. Santa Anna had a passion for cockfighting, a popular form of entertainment in Mexico and Central America during the 19th century.

of managing the nation—his leadership did not seem so bad. Gradually, aided by his supporters in the army and the church, many Mexicans came to conclude that he had done the best he could to defend the nation in a hopeless situation.

When the Conservatives returned to power early in 1853, their leading ideologue and advocate of long-term economic development, Lucas Alamán, conceived of a strategy to buy enough time to implement a strong central government. Santa Anna was to be "elected" president and then recalled from exile.

The disastrous condition of the nation called for drastic action, but this did not mean Conservative political leaders were foolish enough to trust Santa Anna. Before he was allowed to return on April 1, 1853, he agreed to certain stipulations: His term was to be for one year, and Lucas Alamán was to receive the most important

Santa Anna leaves his hacienda in Turbaco, Colombia, to return to Mexico. For a short time, Santa Anna lived the life of a wealthy country gentleman in exile in Turbaco, but he left this life of leisure behind in 1853, when the Conservatives in power invited him back to serve a fifth term as Mexico's president.

The leading Conservative ideologue Lucas Alamán was to a large degree responsible for Santa Anna's 1853 rehabilitation. The hope of Alamán and other Conservatives was that another Santa Anna presidency would buy enough time for them to establish a strong Conservative central government.

post in his cabinet. The other cabinet posts were to be filled with staunch Conservatives also, but Alamán was the one expected to monitor Santa Anna's actions.

On April 20, 1853, Santa Anna took the presidential oath of office for the fifth and last time. He immediately set about implementing the Conservative agenda: Congress and the state legislatures were adjourned; state tax revenue administration and collection was transferred to the central government; freedom of the press was suspended; and a new constitution authorizing a highly centralized government was drafted. In addition, Santa Anna ordered the arrest and exile of political opponents such as Benito Juárez and Melchor Ocampo, both soon to be notable leaders of the Liberal movement called La Reforma.

To ensure the support of the army, Santa Anna lavished the military with attention and funds. The total number of soldiers almost doubled to 90,000 men, and the Order of Guadalupe, originally created by Iturbide, was revived. To win the spurs of a knight in the highly prestigious Order of Guadalupe, one had to pander to Santa Anna. Loyalty, not accomplishment, was the only criterion for selection.

If Santa Anna had served only a year in office and remained merely a figurehead for Alamán's carefully conceived national development programs, perhaps he might be remembered today in Mexico as one of the country's great political leaders. But fate intervened; Lucas Alamán died on June 2, 1853. With his death, the most important brake on Santa Anna's egotistical usurpation of Conservative goals for personal power was suddenly gone. Alamán's death was a tragedy for Santa Anna as well as for Mexico. Alamán provided the balance Santa Anna needed to check his inclination to seize the moment for short-term personal gain rather than for long-term national development.

Santa Anna wasted no time in taking advantage of the opportunity provided by the confusion the death of Alamán caused among Conservatives. The capable, principled Conservative offi-

Santa Anna takes the oath of office to serve a fifth term as president of Mexico. Immediately, he set about implementing a repressive right-wing agenda: He adjourned Congress and the state legislatures, placed tight controls on the press, and trampled civil liberties at every level.

cials in his cabinet were swiftly replaced with corrupt ones who were loyal to Santa Anna. The results were predictable: The government was soon run solely for the enrichment of Santa Anna and his cronies. Public expenditures soared, and the treasury was burdened with a huge foreign debt to finance the exorbitant deficit spending. The transformation of Santa Anna from president to demagogue was completed in October, when he announced that opponents of his regime would be arrested by his newly organized secret police and would then be tried. Those convicted of disloyalty were to be shot immediately. Anyone who failed to report over-hearing someone who made a hostile remark about the administration could also be arrested and fined.

December 1853 marked both the zenith and the nadir of Santa Anna's last brief period as Mexico's leader. To negate the original deal with the Conservatives that he serve only one year, Santa Anna orchestrated various proclamations, mostly by military officers, endorsing him as the man to become emperor of Mexico. On December 16, 1853, Santa Anna demurely declined the title of emperor but accepted that of His Most Serene Highness (*Su Alteza Serenísima*). Along with his new title, Santa Anna extended his term indefinitely and assumed the right to name his successor. Santa Anna's career had now come full circle. Thirty-one years before, he had helped establish His Highness Agustín Iturbide as emperor. Now he had more power than his predecessor.

The first act of His Most Serene Highness paved the way for his overthrow. Having run out of ways to increase taxes and to borrow money, Santa Anna decided to sell more of Mexico to the United States. On December 30, 1853, he signed a treaty with U.S. minister to Mexico James Gadsden by which Mexico sold the area south of the Gila River, known as the Mesilla Valley, to the United States for $10 million. The United States wanted the area along its southwestern border for a proposed southern transcontinental railroad.

To calm the storm of controversy in Mexico that arose over the Gadsden Purchase, Santa Anna claimed that he had no choice: The United States would have taken the area by force if he had not agreed to its sale. "The Government in Washington," he said, "with knife in hand, was planning to cut still another piece from the body it had just mutilated so horribly, and was threatening another invasion. In the deplorable condition of the country a break with the colossus seemed like a catastrophe to me, so I adopted the measure which patriotism and prudence dictated—a peaceful settlement." In other words, he argued, at least he managed to get Mexico a fair price. The tactic did not work. Critics successfully pointed out that the real reason for the sale was Santa Anna's desperate need for money to maintain his military support and extravagant spending.

The remainder of what was to be his brief time in office was marked by personal hedonism and debauchery on a massive scale. The actions of the 60 year old with the wife one-third his age appear to have been prompted by a compulsive need to prove his sexual prowess. His penchant for mistresses degenerated into a steady stream of young women willing to indulge his vanity for large sums of money, and his gambling became obsessive.

Santa Anna's need for adulation, his condolence of corruption, his intolerance of dissent, his sale of Mexican territory to the United States, and the huge increase in taxes he instituted came crashing down on him on March 1, 1854, when a new revolt began with the announcement of the Plan of Ayutla by a Liberal leader. It called for an end to Santa Anna's regime and the convening of a national congress to write a new liberal constitution.

Two weeks later, Santa Anna led a large army out of Mexico City on a leisurely march to crush the rebellion centered at Acapulco. His policy of shooting captured rebels and burning every village suspected of furnishing supplies to the rebels cost him much more political support than it gained. When his men finally arrived at Acapulco, a halfhearted effort to storm the well-fortified position was repulsed. Rather than remain in increasingly hostile rebel territory, Santa Anna declared victory and marched his men back to Mexico City.

Santa Anna's camp bed. Increasingly troubled by popular discontent with his corrupt and repressive regime, Santa Anna was forced to return to the battlefield numerous times during the mid-1850s to put down a series of armed insurrections.

   Although the expedition to Acapulco was officially treated as a success, Santa Anna realized the precariousness of his position. To bolster support, he tried to correct the most flagrant abuses of his administration and declared that the people would have a chance to show their preference through a national referendum on December 1, 1854. The referendum asked: Should Santa Anna remain in office, or should he transfer power to someone else? Each voter was asked to declare publicly how he felt by signing a positive or negative registration book. Once the votes were counted and his continued rule was overwhelmingly approved, Santa Anna promptly ordered the arrest of everyone who had voted against him.

After one last unsuccessful military effort in May and June of 1855 to quell the rising tide of support for his overthrow, Santa Anna realized that he could not save the situation. On August 9, 1855, he appointed a triumvirate to take temporary charge of the government and then announced his abdication. A week later, he and his family boarded a vessel at Antigua for a third journey into "permanent" exile.

Santa Anna's last, brief term as leader of Mexico was not all negative: The army was modernized; public education, under Jesuit control, was improved; the Department of Public Works was created to encourage the growth of new industries; and roads and telegraph lines were built. But in the end, Santa Anna's fifth term, like his others, was extremely corrupt and driven by his extraordinary vanity.

Realizing that he could no longer hold on to power, Santa Anna and his family fled Mexico and settled briefly in Cuba, then Colombia, and then St. Thomas in the Virgin Islands. Although in his sixties, Santa Anna was not ready to retire; he wanted to return to a position of power in Mexico.

CHAPTER 7

Betrayal

Santa Anna's journey into exile in 1855 marked the end of an era. His time of being the archetype for the Latin American curse known as *personalismo*—the discarding of constitutions, political parties, and ideals in favor of personal rule by a caudillo and his lackeys—was over. He was never to return to lead Mexico again.

After a short stay in Havana, Santa Anna returned to his hacienda near Turbaco, Colombia. The 61-year-old exile had many friends in Colombia and might have remained there for the rest of his life except for the personal implications of a local revolution. When the new Colombian caudillo, Tomás Cipriano de Mosquera, threatened to confiscate his hacienda in 1858, Santa Anna decided it was time to leave the country until a more favorable government returned to power.

From Colombia, Santa Anna moved to St. Thomas in the Virgin Islands. He did not expect to reside in the West Indies for long. The Liberals and the Conservatives were fighting again in Mexico, and early Conservative victories in 1858 gave him reason to feel optimistic. If he could get back to Mexico while a Conservative government was in charge, perhaps he could win the presidency again. At least he would have a good chance to successfully reclaim title to his confiscated haciendas.

But times had changed in Mexico. The Liberals turned the tide of battle in their favor in the summer of 1859 by enacting a series of reform laws. Their objective was to control the economic power of the church—Mexico's biggest single landholding, financial, and banking institution—and establish a secular republic.

Instead of trying to understand the new source of power the Liberals had tapped, Santa Anna concluded that the Conservatives just needed foreign support. Because France was the most likely place to obtain aid, the Hero of Tampico immediately began exploring how he could play a role in helping Napoléon III install the European prince, Ferdinand Maximilian Joseph, as emperor of Mexico.

Ferdinand Maximilian Joseph. During the early 1860s, Santa Anna schemed with the French to make Maximilian emperor of Mexico. The plan was for Santa Anna to become one of three regents to rule Mexico during an interim period so that Maximilian could be securely installed.

By 1863, Santa Anna's efforts to ingratiate himself with the French appeared successful. Mexican Conservatives working with the French agreed to include Santa Anna as one of the three regents designated to rule Mexico until Maximilian became emperor. In return for this service and for escorting Maximilian to Mexico City, Santa Anna was to receive a salary equal to his last year as president of Mexico as well as the titles duke of Veracruz and duke of Tampico.

Whether this was just another of Santa Anna's cunning efforts to take advantage of a foreign power or he was genuinely guilty of treason will never be known. Santa Anna's enemies prevented him from playing a major role in the betrayal of his country. When the French seized control of Mexico, Juan Nepomuceno Almonte, a politically ambitious former aide who had once served as Santa Anna's interpreter, succeeded in having Santa Anna removed from the regency triumvirate. Then, as one of the two remaining designated regents, Almonte issued secret orders to the French forces: Santa Anna was not to be allowed to participate in any political activities upon his return to Mexico.

Santa Anna should have dashed to Mexico as soon as the French seized control of Mexico. Such an impetuous move, exactly the kind of action he would have taken in his youth, might have enabled him to overcome local opposition to his return to power. Instead, he waited until the French government initiated its plan to install Maximilian as emperor of Mexico before boarding a British packet sailing to Veracruz. The delay provided Almonte with enough time to solidify his position of influence in the regency at Santa Anna's expense.

When Santa Anna arrived at Veracruz on February 28, 1864, he was surprised and confused by a visit from a French officer. Before he could disembark, the befuddled Santa Anna was required to sign a statement, written in French, that made him promise to support Maximilian and "to abstain from all political demonstration and to do nothing, be it written or verbal, that would make my return to my country be other than as a simple citizen."

The next day, almost ten years after he had fled into exile, Santa Anna was warmly received by the people of Veracruz. Although incapacitated by an attack of dysentery, Santa Anna still managed to issue a proclamation on March 3, encouraging Mexicans to support Maximilian and announcing his willingness to serve in the new emperor's government.

The proclamation gave Almonte just the evidence he needed to convince the French that Santa Anna could not be trusted to keep his word: Less than a week had passed since he had sworn not to make any public statements. True, this proclamation had been in support of Maximilian, but what if he changed his mind? Obviously, Santa Anna was not about to accept life as a simple citizen.

On March 7, the French commander informed Santa Anna that he could not remain in Mexico; he had broken his pledge by making a public proclamation. Santa Anna protested that his proclamation had merely been a local message in support of Maximilian. When this excuse did not work, he claimed that he deserved another chance because he could not read French. The matter was a case of miscommunication, he claimed, rather than any kind of intentional effort to draw attention to himself.

Santa Anna's pleas had no effect. At 4:00 P.M. on March 12, 1864, the French commandant of Veracruz escorted him on board a vessel bound for Cuba. The situation was so absurd—his deportation was the result of his being overly enthusiastic in his support of Maximilian—that Santa Anna could not help laughing with his friends about what was happening. He even teased the French commandant by showing him a welcome letter he had just received from the government praising his support. Although it was postmarked before his deportation order, it had just been delivered. The French commandant read both letters, carefully compared the postmarks, and then carried out his orders. After less than two weeks in Mexico, Santa Anna was forced to return to exile.

At first, upon his return to St. Thomas, Santa Anna believed that Maximilian would realize a mistake had been made and recall him to Mexico. But when Maximilian never issued an invitation,

Santa Anna abandoned the Conservatives and announced a new-found commitment to the Liberal goal of a federal republic. Within a year of his proclamation in Veracruz in which he had praised Maximilian, Santa Anna was now condemning him. In January 1865, he wrote: "Down with the Empire! Long live the Republic!"

It was the same pattern Santa Anna had followed at the start of his political career: First supporting Iturbide's effort to become emperor and then helping overthrow him within a year. Only this time, despite his eagerness to organize and lead an army against the French, he would never get the chance. Like France and the United States, the Liberals had learned their lesson: They were not about to make the mistake of trusting Santa Anna again.

To everyone but himself, Santa Anna had become irrelevant. The battle for control of Mexico was now between Benito Juárez, a true national hero committed to social and economic reform, and a naive foreign aristocrat, Maximilian, installed militarily by the French. Santa Anna was fading from the tapestry of Mexican affairs.

Santa Anna, the Clerical Dictatorship, and the Reform of 1857, *by the 20th-century Mexican painter Diego Rivera. Santa Anna is pictured in uniform, chumming with the clerics, while Benito Juárez (top center) and his fellow reformers look on disapprovingly.*

In 1866, Santa Anna so desperately wanted to regain control of Mexico that he was vulnerable to a scam perpetrated on him by Dario Mazuera, who, presenting himself as a would-be Santa Anna biographer, persuaded the aging Mexican that he had U.S. support for an invasion of Mexico.

CHAPTER 8

Deceit and Despair

In early January 1866, while sailing the Caribbean on vacation, U.S. secretary of state William H. Seward arranged to meet informally with Santa Anna while he was in St. Thomas. Although Seward said very little during their meeting and promised nothing, Santa Anna concluded that the visit meant there was a good possibility he could secure support for an expedition to overthrow Maximilian if he traveled to the United States. This unfounded illusion caused Santa Anna to lose his life's savings in a complicated scam perpetrated by a Colombian swindler named Dario Mazuera.

Mazuera managed to gain Santa Anna's confidence by pretending to be interested in writing a sympathetic biography. Once Santa Anna told him that he had met with Seward, Mazuera had the bait he needed to get the old man to write checks: He convinced Santa Anna, through forged letters and fictitious meetings he claimed to have had with U.S. president Andrew Johnson and Seward while on a trip to the United States, that he had secured U.S. support for an invasion. All Santa Anna had to do was purchase and outfit a ship, hire sailors and a handful of soldiers, and travel to the United States to work out the final invasion details before millions of U.S. dollars would be placed at his disposal.

Santa Anna paid all the bills Mazuera presented to him without making any effort to determine how his money was being spent. What Mazuera told him matched what he wanted so desperately to believe that he failed to verify Mazuera's claims until he traveled to the United States himself in May 1866. Then, too late to save any of his money, he learned that Mazuera had lied. The con man had never met with Seward or the president, nor had he used the money Santa Anna had given him to pay for a ship and soldiers.

As soon as Mazuera learned that Santa Anna had discovered his deception, he disappeared, as did the other participants in the scam. Santa Anna was left stranded in New York with so many creditors demanding payments that he had to use the rest of his fortune to pay lawyers fees to prove his innocence. One year after his arrival, the bitterly disappointed Santa Anna left the United States on March 22, 1867, aboard a U.S. vessel. Although he said he was returning to St. Thomas, he actually sailed to Veracruz to see what he could do to regain power in the wake of the collapse of Maximilian's aborted attempt to establish a monarchy. He still expected, at age 73, to be able to lead a Conservative movement that would gain enough momentum to overcome the radical government of Benito Juárez. Four days after he set sail, the state of Tamaulipas formally recognized Santa Anna as head of the Mexican armies and as interim president.

As soon as he arrived in Veracruz harbor on June 3, Santa Anna took up residence in the castle at San Juan de Ulúa. Initially, events seemed to follow the old familiar script that had worked so well for him in the past. While his supporters in Mexico began whipping up support for him, Santa Anna released a proclamation announcing his readiness to serve his country and reminding his countrymen that he, as one of the few surviving members of the war of independence, had "planted the tree of liberty" and then "watered" it with his own blood.

The one thing Santa Anna had not counted on was the opposition of the United States. On the night of June 7, the evening before he was to land in Veracruz to launch his revolution against the Juárez government, the American naval commander stationed there, acting on orders from Washington, D.C., took him into custody. When Santa Anna protested his transfer from the *Virginia* to the U.S. warship *Tacony*, the American commander replied that he "would take him if he had to break the other leg of the damned old scoundrel." The official explanation for this action was to protect him from assassination. The actual reason was the decision of the United States to support the reform movement in Mexico lead by Benito Juárez. The next day, Santa Anna was returned to the *Virginia*, which was then ordered to leave Mexican waters and was followed far out to sea by a U.S. naval vessel.

The disappointed Santa Anna refused to give up. Instead of accepting defeat and quietly returning to the safety of St. Thomas, when the *Virginia* docked at Sisal, a small port on the northwest coast of the Yucatán, he immediately went ashore and reissued his proclamation. The Yucatán proved to be an even less desirable place than Veracruz to land and launch a revolution. The next morning, Santa Anna was arrested by the local authorities. A few days after his imprisonment at Sisal, Santa Anna was transferred to Campeche. Several weeks later, by order of President Juárez, he was transported back to San Juan de Ulúa in Veracruz to stand trial for treason. Santa Anna spent the next several months in a small cell at San Juan de Ulúa with only two chairs and a small table. The prospect of execution (Maximilian had been executed on June 19, 1867) impelled him to write his will and to reflect upon the irony that the city he had liberated as a young man 45 years earlier at the start of his public career was likely to be the last place he would ever see.

When Santa Anna's trial began on October 7 before a military tribunal, the prosecutor's plea for the death penalty was greeted with eager applause by the excited spectators. The prosecution used the trial to dredge up every accumulated injustice Santa Anna was alleged to have inflicted upon Mexico in his long career. The defense rebutted the allegations by reciting an equally long list of his sacrifices on behalf of the nation.

Juárez did not wish to make a martyr of Santa Anna. Perhaps he realized that treating the vain former dictator as an irrelevant old man was a much harsher punishment than sentencing him to death. At the conclusion of the highly publicized trial, the military tribunal ordered Santa Anna to serve eight more years in exile. Just long enough, the court believed, for the discredited old dic-

A mortgage bond issued in New York City by Santa Anna. In later life, the nearly destitute Santa Anna liquidated his properties in Turbaco, Veracruz, and St. Thomas in order to live out his days in reasonable comfort.

tator to die. On November 1, 1867, he was placed aboard a vessel bound for Cuba.

Santa Anna spent a little more than a year at Puerto Plata, in the Dominican Republic, and then settled at Nassau, in the Bahamas. He did not return to St. Thomas, because he needed the money he raised by selling his property there to live on. For the first time in more than 50 years, Santa Anna engaged in no political activity of consequence. He passed his days corresponding with friends, trying to settle old financial debts, and completing his memoirs. When he was specifically excluded from a general amnesty proclamation by order of Juárez in 1870, it appeared that Santa Anna would die in the Bahamas. Fate intervened; Juárez died first.

A page from Santa Anna's memoirs. In October 1867, Santa Anna was arrested and tried for treason. Although many called for the death penalty, in the end Juárez did not want to make a martyr of Santa Anna and spared his life.

Santa Anna works on his memoirs in one of the last photographs taken of him. To some a courageous defender of Mexican independence, to others a traitor and a scoundrel, Santa Anna dominated Mexican politics—for better or for worse—for more than 30 years. He died on June 21, 1876, in Mexico City.

Six days after his 80th birthday, on February 27, 1874, Santa Anna was allowed to return to Mexico. It was a shallow victory and a disappointing homecoming. Only his brother-in-law greeted the now poor, nearly deaf, and almost blind old man at the dock in Veracruz. The realization that the people of Veracruz did not recognize him was a devastating psychological blow. When a physician told him that he could restore his lost vision by surgically removing his cataracts, Santa Anna replied: "If being blind, I suffered so many ingratitudes on returning to my homeland—what would I see if you again returned my sight? No, I do not wish to see; leave me sunk in darkness, I am more tranquil thus."

He moved on to Mexico City. There, in the house he had bought his bride many years before, she unenthusiastically took care of him as he quietly slipped into senility. Visitors noted that he usually sat in an armchair, unwashed and despondent, dressed in dirty clothes. The dysentery that plagued him all his life finally killed him early in the morning on June 21, 1876. He was buried the next day after a solemn ceremony in the Tepeyac cemetery near Guadalupe Hidalgo.

An obituary in the newspaper *El Siglo Diecinueve* expressed the sentiments of the people of Mexico at the time: "The last hours of his life inspire the saddest reflections: The man who controlled millions, who acquired fortune and honors, who exercised an unrestricted dictatorship, has died in the midst of the greatest want, abandoned by all except a few of his friends. . . . A relic of another epoch, our generation remembered him for the misfortunes he brought upon the republic, forgetting the really eminent services he rendered to the nation." The same sentiments express the feelings of contemporary Mexicans. There are no statues or memorials to Antonio López de Santa Anna in Mexico today.

Chronology

Feb. 21, 1794	Born Antonio López de Santa Anna in Jalapa
1810	Becomes a cadet in the Spanish army
1811–21	Earns distinction and promotion while serving in numerous campaigns against rebels
1821–22	Joins rebels and captures Veracruz for independence movement
1822–24	Supports Iturbide and accepts promotion to brigadier general; leads effort to overthrow Iturbide and to establish a federal republic
1825–27	Retires temporarily from direct political involvement
1828–29	Participates in overthrowing the elected government; becomes a national hero by defeating Spanish invasion effort at Tampico
1829–32	Retires again from direct political involvement
1832–35	Leads successful revolt; becomes president; abandons Liberal party for Conservative party

1835–37	Leads disastrous campaign to crush Texas rebellion; captured and imprisoned; after traveling to Washington, D.C., to secure his release, returns to Mexico
1838–39	Loses most of his left leg in battle to drive an occupying French force from Veracruz; becomes president for the second time
1841–45	Serves a third term as president; exiled after successful Liberal rebellion
1846–48	Returns to Mexico to lead efforts to halt U.S. invasion; becomes president for the fourth time; defeated at battles of Buena Vista, Cerro Gordo, and Molino del Rey; exiled after fall of Mexico City
1853–55	Elected to fifth and last term as president; fails to unite nation; exiled after successful Liberal rebellion
Feb. 28, 1864	Returns to Mexico in unsuccessful bid to help Maximilian become emperor; expelled by French on March 12
1866–67	Loses personal fortune in a misguided effort to secure U.S. aid for invasion of Mexico; imprisoned; tried for treason; exiled for fifth and last time
1867–74	Exile in Havana, Puerto Rico, and Nassau (in the Bahama Islands)
1874–76	Allowed to return to Mexico; dies in Mexico City on June 21, 1876

Further Reading

Acuna, Rodolfo. *Occupied America: A History of Chicanos.* New York: HarperCollins, 1987.

Barker, Eugene H. "President Jackson and the Texas Revolution." *The American Historical Review* XII, no. 4 (July 1907): 788–809.

———."The United States and Mexico, 1835–1837." *The Mississippi Valley Historical Review* I, no. 1 (June 1914): 3–30.

Benson, Nettie Lee. "The Plan of Casa Mata." *The Hispanic American Historical Review* XXV, no. 1 (February 1945): 45–56.

Callcott, Wilfrid Hardy. *Santa Anna: The Story of an Enigma Who Once Was Mexico.* Norman: University of Oklahoma Press, 1936.

Castañeda, Carlos E. "Relations of General Scott with Santa Anna." *The Hispanic American Historical Review* XXIX, no. 4 (November 1949): 455–73.

Cockcroft, James D. *Intellectual Precursors of the Mexican Revolution, 1900–1913. Latin American Monographs,* no. 14 (1969).

————. *Mexico.* New York: Monthly Review Press, 1990.

Crawford, Ann Fears, ed. *The Eagle: The Autobiography of Santa Anna.* Austin: Pemberton Press, 1967.

Hanighen, Frank C. *Santa Anna: The Napoléon of the West.* New York: Coward-McCann, 1934.

Hutchinson, C. Alan. "Valentín Gómez Farías and the Movement for the Return of General Santa Anna to Mexico in 1846." In *Essays in Mexican History*, edited by Thomas E. Cotner and Carlos E. Castañeda. Austin: Institute of Latin American Studies, 1958.

Jones, Oakah L. *Santa Anna.* New York: Twayne, 1936.

Priestly, James. "Santa Anna in Texas: A Mexican Viewpoint." *Southwestern Historical Quarterly* LXII, no. 4 (April 1959): 489–512.

Ragan, John. *Emiliano Zapata.* New York: Chelsea House, 1989.

Raines, C. W. "Life of Antonio López de Santa-Anna," *The Texas Magazine* I, no. 1 (May 1896): 1–16, through III, no. 6 (December 1897): 325–30.

Robertson, William S. "French Intervention in Mexico in 1838." *The Hispanic American Historical Review* XXIV, no. 2 (May 1944): 222–52.

Rummel, Jack. *Mexico.* New York: Chelsea House, 1990.

Santa Anna, Antonio López de. *The Eagle: The Autobiography of Santa Anna.* Edited by Ann Fears Crawford, translated by Sam Guyler and Jaime Platon. Austin: Pemberton Press, 1967.

Singletary, Otis. *The Mexican War.* Chicago: University of Chicago Press, 1960.

PICTURE CREDITS

Index

STEVEN O'BRIEN taught high school social studies in Massachusetts for nearly 20 years. He holds an M.A. in history from the University of Connecticut as well as a certificate of advanced study and a Ph.D. from Harvard University. The author of *Alexander Hamilton* in the Chelsea House series WORLD LEADERS—PAST AND PRESENT, his writing has appeared in the *New York Times Magazine* and other publications. He is currently headmaster at the American Community School of Athens in Greece.

RODOLFO CARDONA is professor of Spanish and comparative literature at Boston University. A renowned scholar, he has written many works of criticism, including *Ramón, a Study of Gómez de la Serna and His Works* and *Visión del esperpento: Teoría y práctica del esperpento en Valle-Inclán*. Born in San José, Costa Rica, he earned his B.A. and M.A. from Louisiana State University and received a Ph.D. from the University of Washington. He has taught at Case Western Reserve University, the University of Pittsburgh, the University of Texas at Austin, the University of New Mexico, and Harvard University.

JAMES COCKCROFT is currently a visiting professor of Latin American and Caribbean studies at the State University of New York at Albany. A three-time Fulbright scholar, he earned a Ph.D. from Stanford University and has taught at the University of Massachusetts, the University of Vermont, and the University of Connecticut. He is the author or coauthor of numerous books on Latin American subjects, including *Neighbors in Turmoil: Latin America*, *The Hispanic Experience in the United States: Contemporary Issues and Perspectives*, and *Outlaws in the Promised Land: Mexican Immigrant Workers and America's Future*.